First published in Great Britain in 1981
by Octopus Books Limited

This edition published in 1985 by
Treasure Press
59 Grosvenor Street
London W1

© 1981 Octopus Books Limited

ISBN 1 85051 056 3

Printed in Hong Kong

Contents

B. Mitchell

This is Magic

This book has been specially written for people who know nothing about conjuring but who would like to know how to do a few tricks.

There is nothing really difficult about the tricks explained in this book. You do not need any previous experience or special training to perform them. All you need is the ability to read the instructions, and the patience to practise each trick until you can do it perfectly.

As you read through the secrets explained in this book, you may be rather disappointed to discover that magicians are not really magicians after all. They are merely ordinary people pretending to be magicians. If true magic were possible, it would be wonderful. It would be nice to be able to make people disappear, to produce money from the air, or to change water into wine. But none of this is really possible. A magician pretends that it is. And if you want to be a magician, you have to pretend that what you do is really magic.

The great English magician David Devant once said that a magician is really only an actor playing the part of a magician. That is what you must try to become. And your acting must be so good that everyone will believe that you possess unusual powers.

There is a large number of tricks in this book. Do not try to learn them all at once. The best thing to do is to read straight through the book first to get some idea of the principles of conjuring. Then select just two or three tricks that appeal to you and learn them thoroughly. It is much better to do a few tricks well than to know hundreds of tricks and not be able to perform any of them convincingly. So, just select a few and learn them, then practise them, and then perform them as often as you can. Only when you can do these tricks perfectly should you try to add some of the other tricks to your repertoire.

All of the tricks in this book can be done with things that are found around the house or which are readily obtainable. Where a special piece of apparatus has to be used you will be told how you can make it yourself.

When you read through some of the tricks, you may say 'That is so simple no one will be fooled by it.' But as someone who has performed magic for many years on stage, television, and even on radio, I can tell you that some of the simplest methods are responsible for some of the most baffling tricks. And

anyway, the method used to perform a trick is not really important. It is the way that you present it that is the most important aspect of any trick.

This book can only tell you how certain tricks are done—it cannot teach you how to become a magician. The real art of magic consists of your personality and how you present the tricks you learn. A trick performed by a certain magician may be little more than a puzzle but the very same trick performed by another magician, who brings to it his own personality and his own original touches, may be a miracle. It is really up to you whether you become a mere presenter of tricks or a real magician.

Each time you learn a new trick see if you can improve it a little, perhaps by saying a few jokes, altering the way the trick is performed, or by changing the objects used for the trick. In this way you will learn how to become a real magician and not just someone who knows how a few tricks are done.

Once people know that you can do some magic you will find you will often be asked to show someone a trick. You must, therefore, be ready to perform at least one trick at a moment's notice. Because of this several of the tricks in this book do not need any special preparation. Provided that you know how to do them and that you have practised them to perfection, you will be ready to show several fantastic tricks without special preparation.

Magic is a fascinating hobby—fascinating for those that practise it and equally fascinating for those that watch. It is rather fun to be able to do a few conjuring tricks. It is even more fun if you decide to take up magic as a hobby.

When you have read this book you may want to learn some more about conjuring. There are a great many books that will help you. Ask at your local library. If they cannot advise you drop me a line care of the publishers. I will be happy to do my best to help you. Magic has proved a fascinating and rewarding hobby for me—I hope that you will find it equally exciting.

Peter Eldin

PETER ELDIN

Nifty Tricks

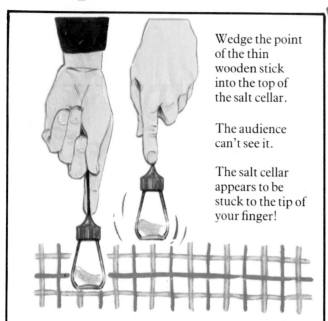

Wedge the point of the thin wooden stick into the top of the salt cellar.

The audience can't see it.

The salt cellar appears to be stuck to the tip of your finger!

Salt in Suspension ▲

When you touch the top of a salt cellar it clings to your fingertip. 'It must be magic,' all your friends will say.

What they do not see is that you have a thin wooden stick hidden behind your finger. The point of the stick is wedged into the opening in the top of the salt cellar. To people watching from the front it looks as if the cellar is stuck to your finger.

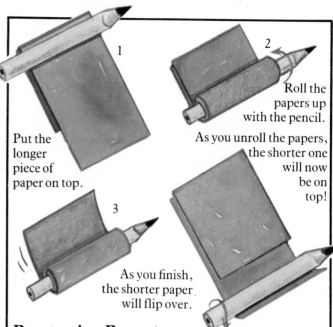

1. Put the longer piece of paper on top.

2. Roll the papers up with the pencil.
As you unroll the papers, the shorter one will now be on top!

3. As you finish, the shorter paper will flip over.

Penetrating Paper ▲

For this trick you need two sheets of paper, one slightly longer than the other. Use paper of different colours—or paper money.

Place the short sheet on the table. Put the larger sheet on top of it.

Put a pencil at one end of the papers and start rolling them up together.

When you come to the end the short paper will 'flip' over. As soon as this happens start unrolling the papers.

The papers have now changed places with the short one on top and the larger underneath. What an amazing trick!

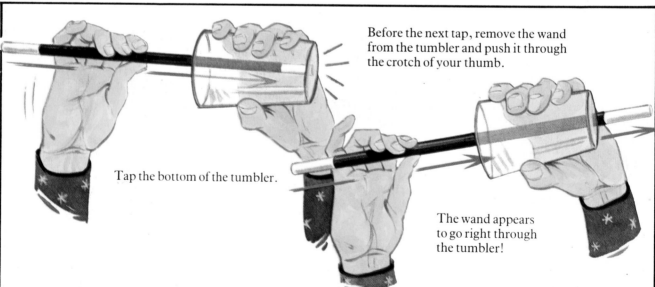

Tap the bottom of the tumbler.

Before the next tap, remove the wand from the tumbler and push it through the crotch of your thumb.

The wand appears to go right through the tumbler!

Through the Bottom ▲

For this trick you will need a magic wand. This is simply a stick painted black with white ends. (See page 10). You will also need a glass tumbler.

Hold the tumbler in your left hand, the wand in your right. Tap the wand on the bottom of the tumbler (on the inside) a couple of times. As you go to make the third tap you remove the wand and place it behind the tumbler through the crotch of your left thumb. You continue pushing until the wand appears beyond the base of the tumbler. To the audience it appears that the wand has gone right through.

Put your finger into your ear.

Run your fingertip along the water's surface.

The pepper will stay divided.

Sprinkle pepper on to the water.

Pepper Separation ▲

Get a glass of water and sprinkle some pepper all over the surface of the water.

While you are talking about the amazing trick you are about to perform casually put your finger into your ear. This will enable you to get a thin layer of wax on your fingertip.

Now run your fingertip along the surface of the water. Much to everyone's surprise the pepper will divide along the imaginary line.

Push the hanky to the bottom.

Put the beaker upside down in the water. The hanky will stay dry!

◄ Dry Hanky

How can you put a hanky under water without it getting wet?

This is how a magician can do it.

Push the hanky into the bottom of a beaker. Now turn the beaker upside down and push it straight down into a bowl of water.

Wrap your fingers right over your left hand.

Keep the handle hidden.

Secretly put your left little finger to the front of the handle.

Move your hands backwards and forwards while pretending to press hard on the table. It will look as though the spoon is bending.

Spoon Bender ▲

Pick up a spoon from the dinner table. Hold the handle tightly in your left fist. Wrap the fingers of your right hand over the left hand.

Secretly put your left little finger to the front of the handle.

Put the bowl of the spoon on the table and press. Pretend to be pressing really hard. At the same time move your hands up to a vertical position. The handle of the spoon is now sticking out at the back of your hands but your wrists and arms conceal it from view.

Move the hands backwards and forwards and it will really look as if you are bending the spoon.

Wave your right hand over the spoon and throw the spoon on the table. It is back to normal again.

9

The Magic Wand

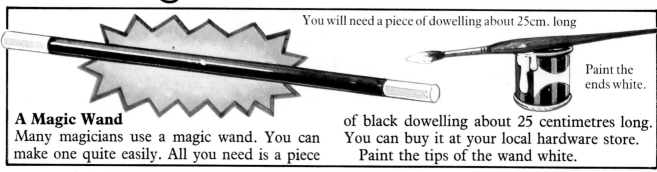

You will need a piece of dowelling about 25cm. long

Paint the ends white.

A Magic Wand

Many magicians use a magic wand. You can make one quite easily. All you need is a piece of black dowelling about 25 centimetres long. You can buy it at your local hardware store. Paint the tips of the wand white.

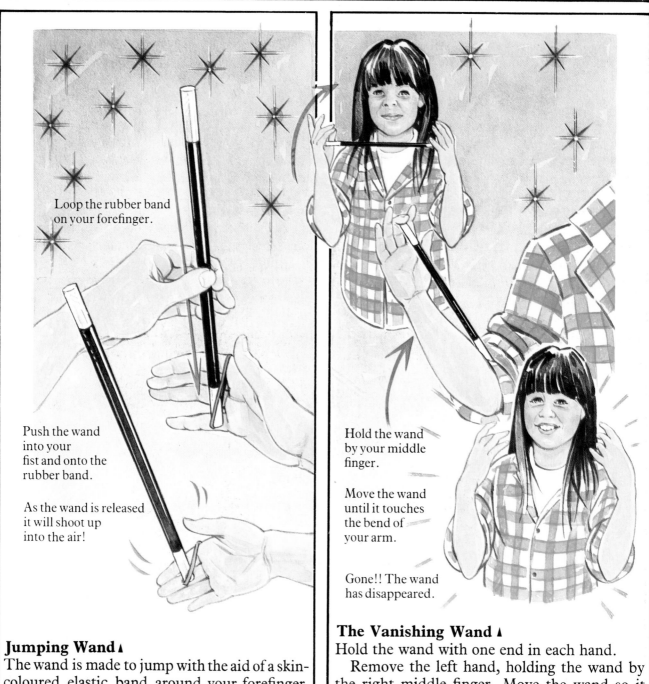

Loop the rubber band on your forefinger.

Push the wand into your fist and onto the rubber band.

As the wand is released it will shoot up into the air!

Hold the wand by your middle finger.

Move the wand until it touches the bend of your arm.

Gone!! The wand has disappeared.

Jumping Wand ▲

The wand is made to jump with the aid of a skin-coloured elastic band around your forefinger.

Push the wand into your fist and against the elastic band. As soon as you release your grip on the wand it will leap into the air. Try to catch it and drop the elastic band.

The Vanishing Wand ▲

Hold the wand with one end in each hand.

Remove the left hand, holding the wand by the right middle finger. Move the wand so it points towards your right arm. Keep the wand moving until it touches the bend in your arm.

Look up in the air and hold both hands up, backs to the audience. The wand has vanished!

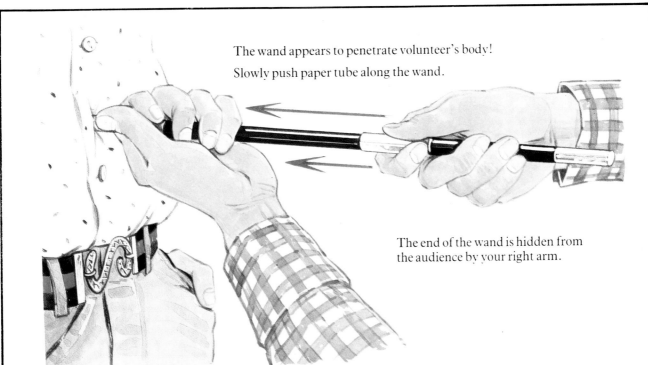

The wand appears to penetrate volunteer's body!

Slowly push paper tube along the wand.

The end of the wand is hidden from the audience by your right arm.

Hole in the Body ▲

When you have made your magic wand get a small piece of white paper and some glue and you can make the equipment for this trick.

Cut the paper to the same length as one of the tips of your wand. Roll the paper around the wand and glue the ends of the paper together. You now have a little paper tube that will slide along the wand.

Get someone up from the audience and ask him to stand facing the front. Touch the end of the wand against his body. Cover the tip with your left hand.

Slowly push the paper tube along the wand. It looks as if the wand is being pushed into the person's body. The end of the wand nearest to you is hidden from the audience by your right arm.

When the wand is apparently right into the body start pulling the tube back again. As soon as you reach the end of the wand grip it tighter so the other end is pulled from your left hand.

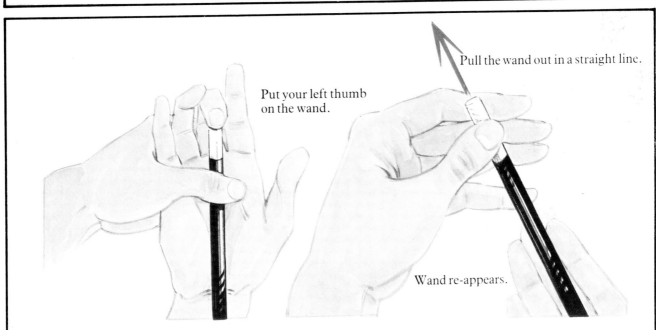

Put your left thumb on the wand.

Pull the wand out in a straight line.

Wand re-appears.

The Wand Reappears ▲

When you make the wand vanish, as in the trick opposite, here is how to get it back again.

The wand is still held by the middle finger and the bend of the arm.

Move both hands inwards so that the left hand is touching the back of the right.

Place your left thumb on the end of the wand. Pull the wand out in a straight line until it is once again held between the hands.

Magic that Mystifies

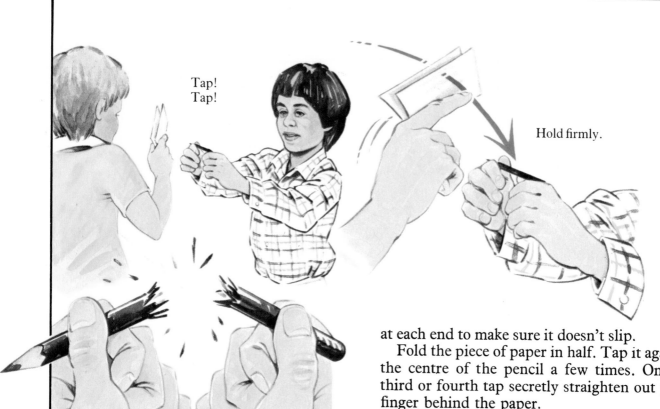

Tap!
Tap!

Hold firmly.

Snap!

at each end to make sure it doesn't slip.

Fold the piece of paper in half. Tap it against the centre of the pencil a few times. On the third or fourth tap secretly straighten out your finger behind the paper.

If you hit the pencil sharply it will break. You will not hurt your finger.

As soon as the pencil has broken curl your finger back into the fist. Allow everyone to examine the paper. They will not be able to discover how the trick is done.

Strong Paper ▲

In this amazing trick you break a wooden pencil using only a piece of paper.

Ask someone to hold the pencil very firmly

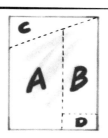
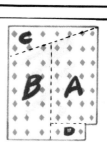
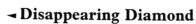

Count the diamonds – one has disappeared!

◄ Disappearing Diamond

Copy the design shown here onto a piece of paper or card very accurately.

Cut the card as shown by the lines.

Show the card to your friends. When they count the diamonds, there are fifty six.

Pick up the various pieces. Wave your hand over them in a mysterious fashion. Now put them back down on the table but with the two large pieces transposed. The piece marked A goes on the right, and the one marked B in the picture goes on the left.

Ask your friends to count the diamonds once again. There are now only fifty five!

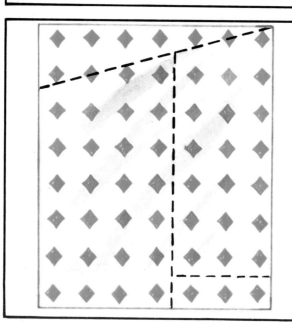

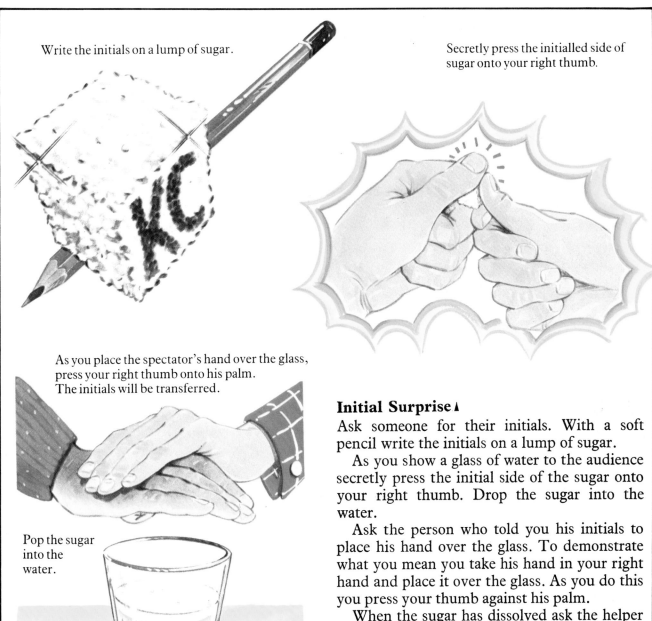

Write the initials on a lump of sugar.

Secretly press the initialled side of sugar onto your right thumb.

As you place the spectator's hand over the glass, press your right thumb onto his palm. The initials will be transferred.

Pop the sugar into the water.

Initial Surprise▲

Ask someone for their initials. With a soft pencil write the initials on a lump of sugar.

As you show a glass of water to the audience secretly press the initial side of the sugar onto your right thumb. Drop the sugar into the water.

Ask the person who told you his initials to place his hand over the glass. To demonstrate what you mean you take his hand in your right hand and place it over the glass. As you do this you press your thumb against his palm.

When the sugar has dissolved ask the helper to turn his hand over. There in the middle of his palm will be his own initials!

Conceal the sponge in your hand.

Squeeze!

Water on the Elbow▲

'You've heard of water on the knee' says the magician as he looks at a spectator who has come onto the stage to help. 'Well you are suffering from water on the elbow.'

As he says this the magician grasps the spectator's right elbow with his right hand and a stream of water pours from it.

Conjuring with Colour

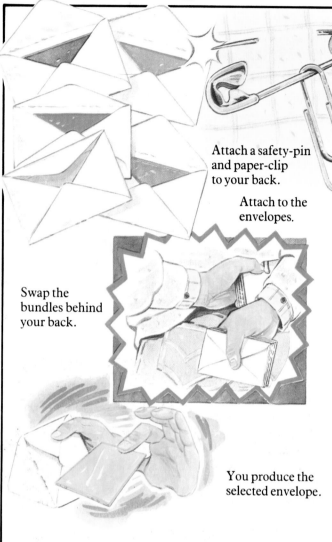

Attach a safety-pin and paper-clip to your back.

Attach to the envelopes.

Give out five more envelopes and pieces of card to the audience.

Swap the bundles behind your back.

You produce the selected envelope.

Colour Magic ⌐

Five pieces of coloured card are each placed into an envelope by a spectator. What the audience do not know is that you have a duplicate set of envelopes with cards inside them. These are arranged in order so you know which is which. They are then pinned to your back under your coat at the back.

Five coloured cards and five envelopes are handed out. The spectators put one card in each envelope and mix them up. As soon as they are returned to you hold them behind your back. While you are asking someone to call out a colour you secretly remove the arranged set of envelopes from the clip and put the mixed up set into the clip.

As soon as someone names a colour you select that envelope from the arranged ones you hold and bring it forward. When the envelope is opened you are seen to be correct.

Colour Separation ►

Take a pack of cards and separate the red cards from the blacks. Bend the red cards slightly inwards. Bend the black cards slightly outwards. Do not overdo this bending. The cards should be bent just enough so you can tell the difference between a red and a black card but so people who do not know the secret will not be able to spot it.

When the time comes to show the trick you deal the cards face down onto the table. They are spread out all over the table so no one can know which are red and which are black.

Ask someone to point to a card and you tell them whether it is red or black. Do this a couple of times and then start picking up the cards as fast as you can calling out 'red' or 'black' each time. Because of the secret bending it is quite easy for you to tell which is which.

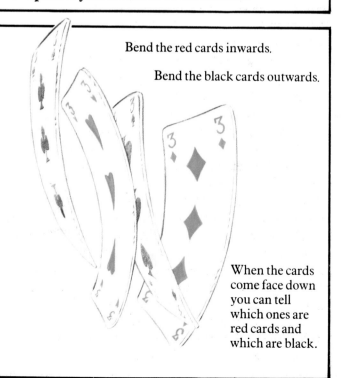

Bend the red cards inwards.

Bend the black cards outwards.

When the cards come face down you can tell which ones are red cards and which are black.

Cut out the centre diamond.

Mark the back so that the colours are in the correct position each time.

Make sure the colour areas are large enough.

Pass a coloured hanky over the ace and secretly move the coloured card with your thumb.

Colourful Diamond ▲

The magician takes an Ace of Diamonds from a pack of cards.

When he passes a green handkerchief over it the central pip changes from red to green. A yellow handkerchief is passed over the card and the pip changes to yellow. Next a blue handkerchief is used and the pip changes to blue. Finally a red handkerchief causes the diamond to return to its normal colour.

This pretty trick is very simple to do. Get an Ace of Diamonds and carefully cut out the centre diamond to make a diamond-shaped hole.

Now all you need is a piece of card with the four colours painted on it. This is held behind the playing card. To change the colour of the diamond the piece of card is moved behind the Ace so that a different colour shows through.

It is a good idea to mark the back of the piece of card and the playing card so you can be certain of moving to the correct position each time.

Passing a handkerchief over the Ace each time conceals the movement of the secret card.

Coloured Thoughts ►

While your back is turned, ask a spectator to hand you any one of a number of coloured felt tipped pens. When you turn back you are able to tell everyone the colour you have been given even though all the pens have been hidden.

When a pen is handed to you turn round to face the audience. Keep the pen behind your back. Secretly remove the cap from the pen and make a small mark on the back of your hand. Put the cap back on.

Still keeping the pen behind your back, bring your empty hand forward and up to your forehead as if concentrating. It is now an easy matter to see the mark on the back of your hand so you know what colour was chosen.

Put on a mysterious voice and then name the colour. At the same time bring the pen into view so everyone can see you are correct.

Make a small mark.

Pins and Clips

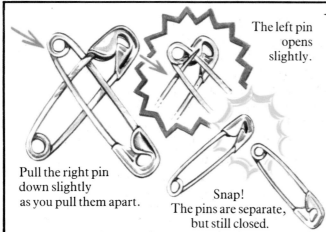

The left pin opens slightly.

Pull the right pin down slightly as you pull them apart.

Snap! The pins are separate, but still closed.

◄ **Pin Penetration**

Pin Penetration

All you need for this trick are two safety pins.

Link the pins together. Now hold them in the position shown in the first picture.

Pull the pins apart sharply and they will separate—but they will still be closed.

It works best if the right pin is pulled downwards slightly as you pull them apart. What really happens is shown in the illustrations. One of the pins is actually pulled open but it then closes again.

Practice this until you can do it every time. Then you can show it to your friends.

Ask two people to hold the two top corners of a large handkerchief or scarf.

Pierce the material very close to the edge and fasten the pin.

Pull the pin quickly.

The material is pulled under the catch of the pin and the pin changes its position on the handkerchief without ripping it.

That's Torn It!

You need a large handkerchief and one of the pins from the last trick for this little miracle.

Ask two people to hold the handkerchief between them. Pin the safety pin near to the top edge. The pin *must* be as shown.

Hold the pin by the small end and pull it quickly to the right. The material will be folded over the catch of the pin and the handkerchief will not be harmed. But it looks as if you are pulling the pin through the material.

When you stop the pin has been moved from its original position but it is still through the handkerchief.

Practise this with an old handkerchief until you can do it properly.

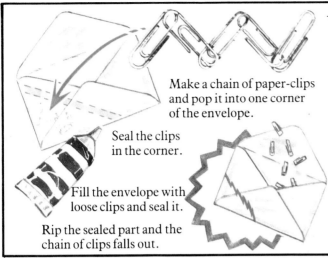

Make a chain of paper-clips and pop it into one corner of the envelope.

Seal the clips in the corner.

Fill the envelope with loose clips and seal it.

Rip the sealed part and the chain of clips falls out.

◄ Chain of Clips

Get some paper clips and link them into a chain. Put the chain into an envelope.

Now put a strip of glue along the inside of the envelope as shown. When the glue has dried tip some paper clips into the envelope.

During your show you pick up the envelope and tip out the loose clips. The audience will assume the envelope is empty.

Drop the clips back and seal the envelope.

Say a magic spell and tap the envelope with your magic wand. Tear the envelope across the bottom right hand corner. Tip the envelope up and the chain will slide out into your hand.

The Magic Clips

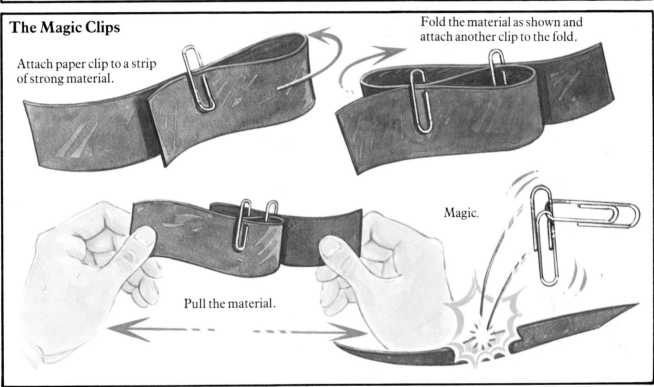

Attach paper clip to a strip of strong material.

Fold the material as shown and attach another clip to the fold.

Pull the material.

Magic.

Ask someone to clip the ace from the back.

Glue 5 cards together with the ace in the middle.

SURPRISE! SURPRISE!

Clipped Card ▲

Glue five old playing cards, including the Ace of Spades, together as shown in the picture.

When the glue has dried hand someone the cards and a paper clip.

Point out that the Ace is in the middle.

Tell him to turn the packet of cards face down and clip on the card he thinks is the ace.

He will naturally clip the middle card.

When he turns the cards face up again he will receive quite a surprise. The clip is not on the ace at all. It is on the end card!

Curious Knots

Flick your hand over.

Let the hanky fall from your hand.

Hold the hanky between these two fingers only as it falls.

A magic knot forms.

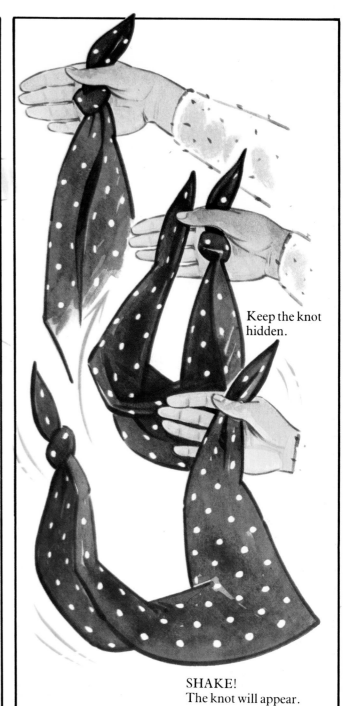

Keep the knot hidden.

SHAKE!
The knot will appear.

Quick Knot ▲

Drape a handkerchief over your hand as shown.

Bend your first and second fingers over and grab the handkerchief at the point marked X.

Allow the rest of the handkerchief to fall from the back of your hand. A knot will now form automatically in the handkerchief.

Appearing Knot ▲

Secretly tie a knot in one corner of a handkerchief and show the handkerchief to your friends. Hold it by the knotted corner so the knot is hidden in your hand.

Place the lowermost corner into your hand with the knotted corner.

Give the handkerchief a shake. Let go of the knotted corner and keep hold of the other.

All you have done is to change the corner you are holding. To your audience it seems that a knot has formed all by itself.

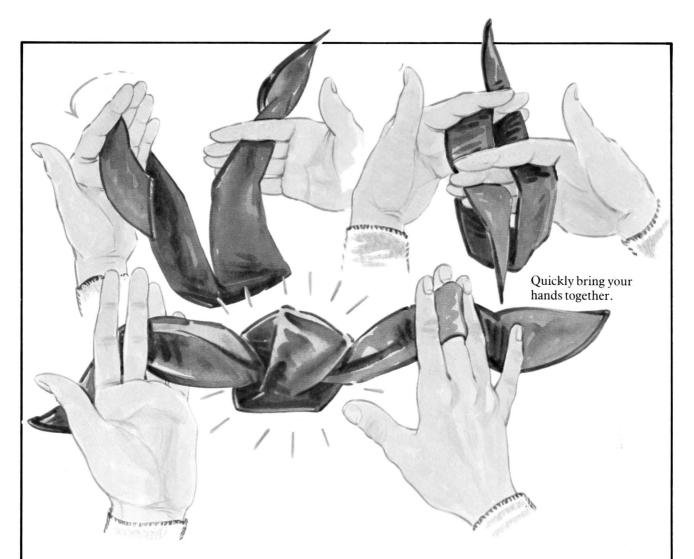

Quickly bring your hands together.

Instant Knot ▲

Hold a handkerchief by two opposite corners. Each corner is held by the first and second fingers of each hand. But the left corner goes through the fingers from front to back and that in the right hand goes from back to front. Look at the pictures to make sure you are holding your handkerchief in the same way.

Quickly bring the hands together. At this point the second and third fingers of the right hand open to take the end of the handkerchief sticking out from the back of the left hand. At the same time the second and third fingers of the left hand grab the right corner sticking out from the front of the right hand.

Pull the hands apart and a knot will be formed in the handkerchief. The pictures show this sequence of moves.

The whole movement is quite easy to do but you must practise it until you can do it quickly and smoothly. It will then seem that you simply shook the handkerchief and a knot formed.

As you put the hanky into your hand secretly tuck the end into an elastic band.

Repeat with another hanky so that the ends are magically joined!

◄ Knot from Nowhere

Before starting your magic act secretly place a small elastic band over your little finger.

When the time comes for this trick pull the band from your finger and hide it in your hand.

Pick up a handkerchief from your table and place it into your hand. Secretly place it into the elastic band at the same time.

Pick up another handkerchief and place this in your hand as well. This is also pushed into the elastic band.

Throw both the handkerchiefs into the air. As they fall catch one of them. The elastic band will hold the two handkerchiefs together.

Conjuring with Cards

Secretly prepare a pack of cards.

◄ Take a Card

Prepare a pack of cards by drawing two or three heavy diagonal pencil lines down one side.

When the time comes to show a trick remove the pack from its case. Spread the cards out and ask someone to take out any card. Ask that person to remember the card he has chosen.

The card is now returned to the pack while the magician's eyes are closed.

You can now find the selected card immediately. If you look at the side of the pack you will see that your pencilled lines are broken. Somewhere else in the pack there will be a card bearing a mark that does not fit in with the lines. Remove it from the pack and take a bow.

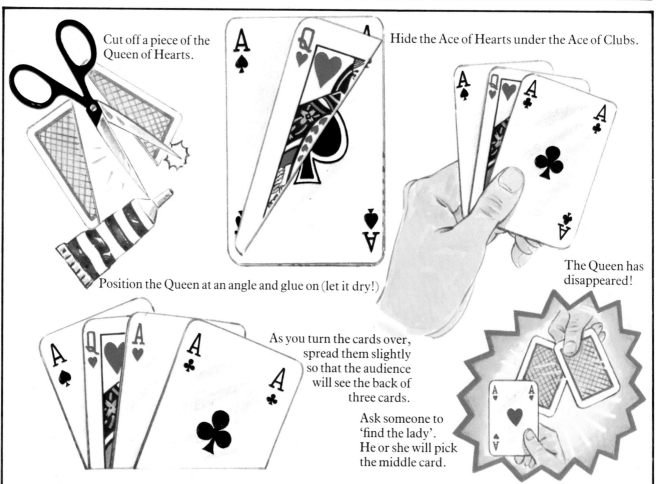

Cut off a piece of the Queen of Hearts.

Hide the Ace of Hearts under the Ace of Clubs.

Position the Queen at an angle and glue on (let it dry!)

The Queen has disappeared!

As you turn the cards over, spread them slightly so that the audience will see the back of three cards.

Ask someone to 'find the lady'. He or she will pick the middle card.

Find the Lady ◣

For this trick you must make a special card. Take a Queen of Hearts and cut a large piece from it. This piece is glued on to the face of an Ace of Spades. Position the Queen at an angle.

You will also need an Ace of Hearts and an Ace of Clubs. Place these two together and hold them on top of the special card. It looks as if you are holding a fan of three cards.

Ask someone to keep an eye on the Queen. Turn the cards over. At the same time spread the cards slightly between your fingers so when the cards are turned over the spectators will still see three cards.

Invite someone to remove the Queen. They will naturally take the centre card. When it is turned over it is not the Queen of Hearts. It is the Ace of Hearts!

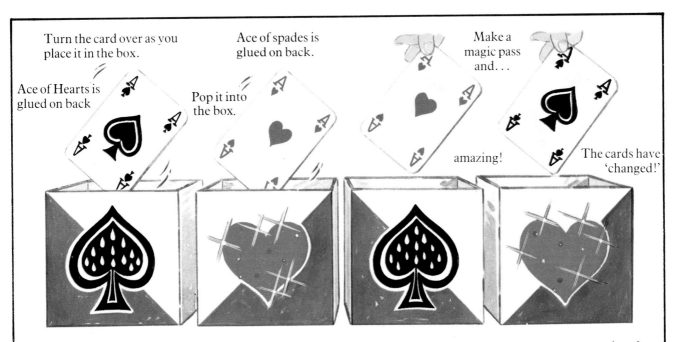

Ace of Hearts is glued on back

Turn the card over as you place it in the box.

Ace of spades is glued on back.

Pop it into the box.

Make a magic pass and...

amazing!

The cards have 'changed!'

Quick Change ▲

The magician shows an Ace of Spades and places it into an empty box. On the front of the box is painted a spade symbol.

He then shows an Ace of Hearts and places this into another empty box. Painted on this box is a heart symbol.

After making a magic pass remove the Ace of Spades from the Heart box. The Ace of Hearts has also changed boxes. On the back of the Ace of Hearts is glued an Ace of Spades and on the back of the Ace of Spades is an Ace of Hearts. All you have to do is to turn each card over as you place it into its box.

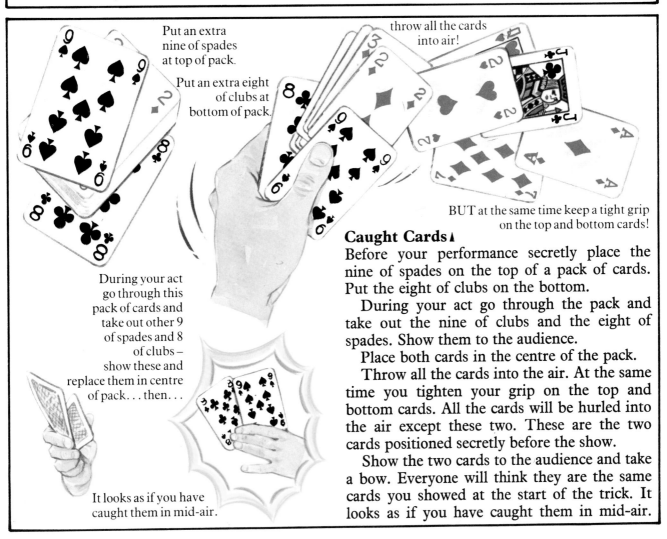

Put an extra nine of spades at top of pack.

Put an extra eight of clubs at bottom of pack.

throw all the cards into air!

During your act go through this pack of cards and take out other 9 of spades and 8 of clubs – show these and replace them in centre of pack...then...

It looks as if you have caught them in mid-air.

BUT at the same time keep a tight grip on the top and bottom cards!

Caught Cards ▲

Before your performance secretly place the nine of spades on the top of a pack of cards. Put the eight of clubs on the bottom.

During your act go through the pack and take out the nine of clubs and the eight of spades. Show them to the audience.

Place both cards in the centre of the pack.

Throw all the cards into the air. At the same time you tighten your grip on the top and bottom cards. All the cards will be hurled into the air except these two. These are the two cards positioned secretly before the show.

Show the two cards to the audience and take a bow. Everyone will think they are the same cards you showed at the start of the trick. It looks as if you have caught them in mid-air.

Conjuring with Coins

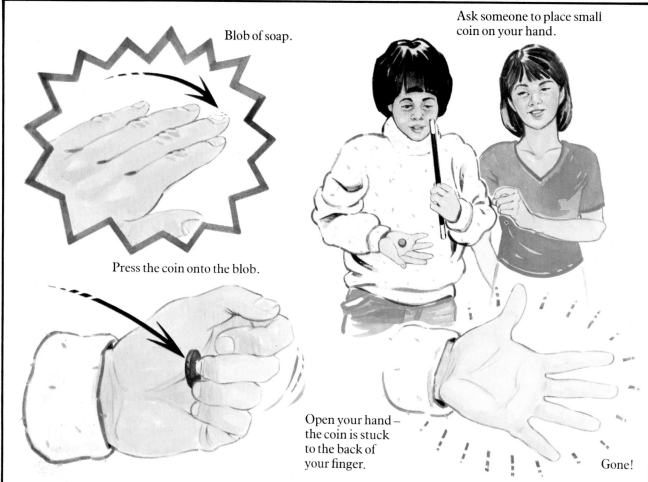

Blob of soap.

Press the coin onto the blob.

Ask someone to place small coin on your hand.

Open your hand – the coin is stuck to the back of your finger.

Gone!

A Quick Vanish ▲

Before showing this trick you must secretly place a small blob of soap on the middle finger nail of your hand.

Hold your hand palm upwards and ask someone to place a small coin on your hand. Make sure that the coin is positioned as shown.

Now close your hand into a fist. You will find that the soaped fingernail comes against the coin. By pressing with the fleshy part of the thumb you can press the coin onto the soap.

If you now open your fingers with the palm of your hand facing the audience the coin will disappear. It is really hidden behind your middle finger—stuck to the soap, but your audience do not realise this.

The Magic Wallet ►

To perform the trick you show the open sheet. The other packet (containing a coin) remains hidden. Close up the empty sheet and secretly turn the whole packet over.

When the paper is now opened the audience will see you have produced a coin.

You can also use this amazing magic wallet to change one coin with another. Secretly put a coin in one side and close it up. Borrow a coin from a member of your audience and fold it into the empty side of the wallet. After you have secretly turned the packet over the wallet is opened. The spectator's coin has changed into one of less value!

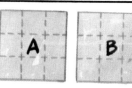

Take two identical sheets of paper. Fold along the dotted lines, and glue area A to area B, back to back.

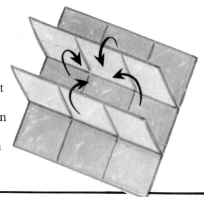

Fold the top sheet inwards to form centre wallet, turn package over and repeat to make an identical wallet.

Invisible Coin

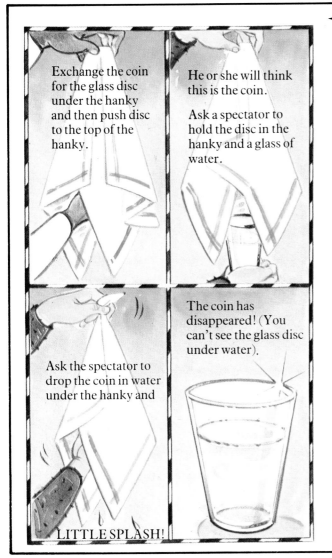

Exchange the coin for the glass disc under the hanky and then push disc to the top of the hanky.

He or she will think this is the coin.

Ask a spectator to hold the disc in the hanky and a glass of water.

Ask the spectator to drop the coin in water under the hanky and

LITTLE SPLASH!

The coin has disappeared! (You can't see the glass disc under water).

To do this trick you will need a glass disc that is more or less the same size as a coin. Ask your local hardware store to make you one.

Conceal the glass disc in your hand. Ask someone for the loan of a coin. At the same time you remove a handkerchief from your pocket. Place the borrowed coin under the handkerchief. It is now an easy matter to exchange the coin for the glass disc. Push the disc up into the handkerchief and ask someone to take hold of it. He will think that it is the borrowed coin.

Now pick up a glass of water that has been standing nearby. While you are doing this you can secretly slip the coin into a convenient pocket.

Place the glass of water under the handkerchief and get the spectator to hold it.

Move to the other side of the room. Ask the spectator to drop the coin (*he* thinks it is a coin) into the glass. As he does this take the real coin from your pocket and put it down in full view. Everyone should be watching the person with the glass so they will not see you do this.

Walk across to the spectator. Take the glass from him and show that the coin has disappeared. As the disc is made of glass no-one will be able to see it.

Say you will make the coin travel across the room. Point to the place where you left the coin and allow someone to go and pick it up.

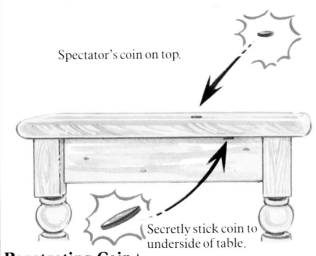

Spectator's coin on top.

Secretly stick coin to underside of table.

WHACK! WHACK!

Penetrating Coin ▲

Put a small dab of wax on a coin and use this to stick the coin under a table. Place another dab of wax on a matchbox or a book and you are ready to perform this baffling feat of magic.

Borrow a coin from a spectator. It must be of the same type as the hidden coin. Place the coin on the table.

Pick up the matchbox and bang it on top of

the coin. This will cause the hidden coin to drop from its hiding place and onto the floor. The coin on the table will stick to the matchbox.

Lift the box to show the coin has gone. Now reach under the table to pick up the coin that has dropped there. At the same time you can secretly remove the coin from the matchbox if you wish. To the audience it seems that you have made a borrowed coin penetrate a table.

Get It Off

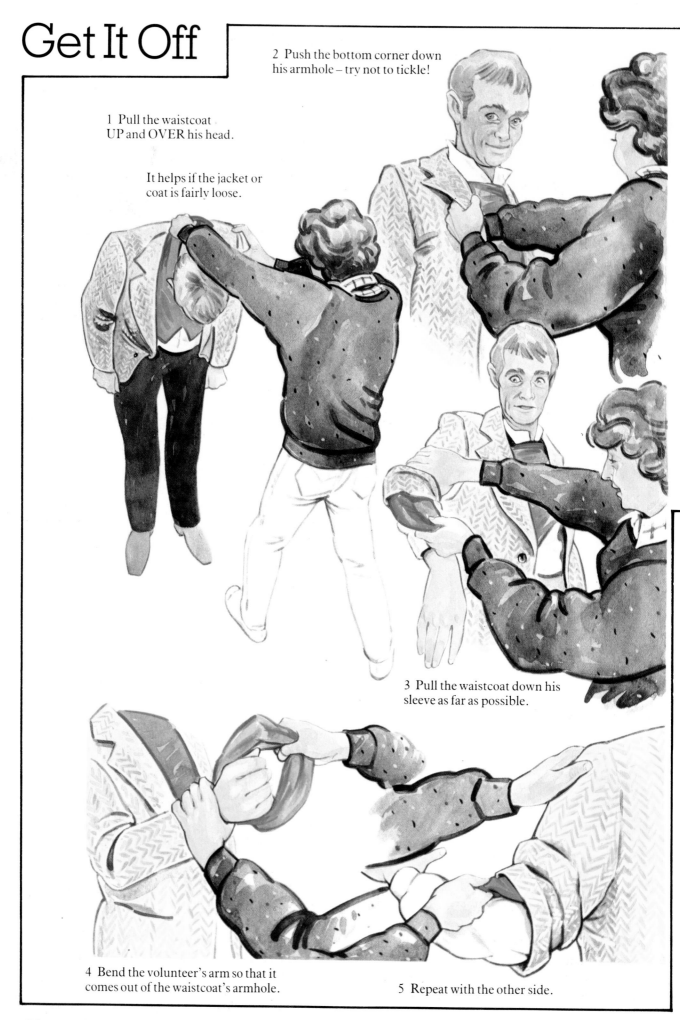

1 Pull the waistcoat UP and OVER his head.

It helps if the jacket or coat is fairly loose.

2 Push the bottom corner down his armhole – try not to tickle!

3 Pull the waistcoat down his sleeve as far as possible.

4 Bend the volunteer's arm so that it comes out of the waistcoat's armhole.

5 Repeat with the other side.

6 You can now take off his waistcoat while his jacket is still on!

◄ Waistcoat Wizardry

Ask a gentleman who is wearing a waistcoat to come up and help you. Say that you are going to remove his waistcoat but not his coat.

It sounds impossible but it is really quite easy if you make the following moves:

Unbutton the waistcoat.

Reach up under the coat at the back and unbuckle the strap on the back of the waistcoat.

Stand in front of your volunteer. Put your hands over his shoulders and into his coat. Pull the top of the waistcoat up and over the man's head. He will have to help by ducking his head.

Now take hold of the right hand bottom corner of the waistcoat. Push it into the armhole of his coat sleeve. Now put your arm up his sleeve and pull the waistcoat down as far as you can.

Ask your volunteer to bend his arm so that it comes out of the armhole of the waistcoat.

You should now be able to pull the waistcoat out of the sleeve.

Now do exactly the same with the other side of the waistcoat.

The waistcoat is now off and the coat has not been removed. Thank your volunteer for being a good sport and then take your bow.

Do up the top two buttons.

Drape the shirt over his shoulders.

Put his wrist through the opening above the cuff and do up the button.

Then replace his tie and jacket.

Seize his shirt and PULL!

Off With His Shirt ▲

Ask someone for his help. You take off his tie and undo the top buttons and the cuffs of his shirt. Then you grab the shirt at the neck and pull it right off over his head. You have taken his shirt off but he still has his coat on!

The person who helps you is in on the trick.

First he drapes the shirt over his shoulders.

The collar and the first two buttons are done up at the front. His arms do not go into the shirt. Put his wrists through the openings just above the cuffs. You can now do the cuffs up in the normal way. When your friend puts on a tie and his jacket the shirt looks quite ordinary.

When you ask him up out of your audience no one will realise that he is your stooge.

Rope and String

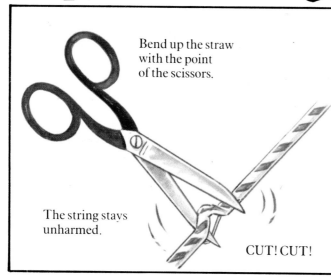

Bend up the straw with the point of the scissors.

The string stays unharmed.

CUT! CUT!

◄ The Magic Straw

Before your performance get a drinking straw and secretly make a slit in it at the centre.

Show the straw to your audience. Do not mention the secret slit. Now thread a length of string through the straw. The easiest way to do this is to have the string attached to a needle. The weight of the needle will pull the string through the straw quite easily.

You now take a pair of scissors and apparently cut through both straw and string. What you really do is to bend the straw with the point of the scissors so the rear blade goes into the slit. You now cut through the straw but the string remains unharmed.

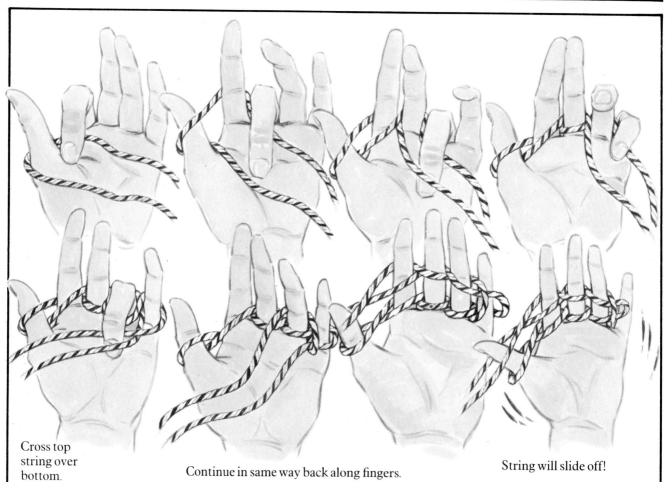

Cross top string over bottom.

Continue in same way back along fingers.

String will slide off!

In a Tangle ▲

Take a long piece of wool, soft rope or string.

Fold it in half and put your thumb in the loop at the centre.

Bend your first finger over the top string and under the lower string. This makes the string wrap itself around the finger.

Do exactly the same with each of the other fingers in turn.

When you pass your little finger *cross the top string over the bottom string* and then continue in the same way back along the fingers. Start with the third finger and end with the thumb.

The string will now look in a tangle.

Slip the loop off your little finger. Pull the string and, much to everyone's astonishment, it slides off the rest of your fingers and is now completely free.

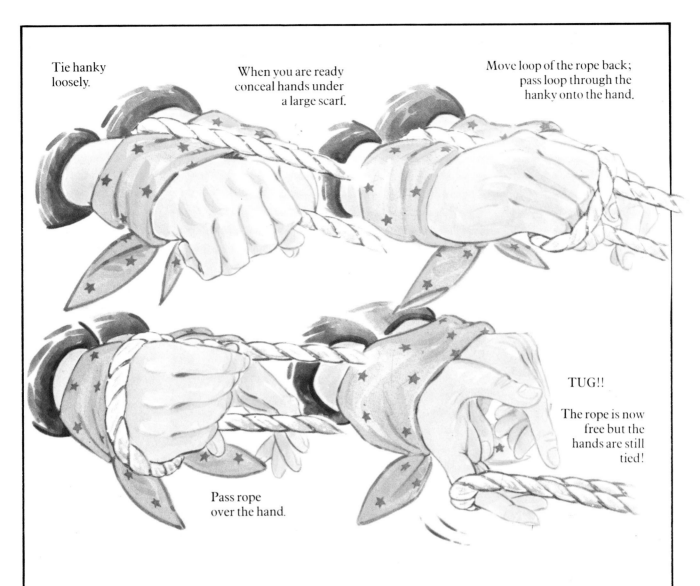

Tie hanky
loosely.

When you are ready
conceal hands under
a large scarf.

Move loop of the rope back;
pass loop through the
hanky onto the hand.

TUG!!

The rope is now
free but the
hands are still
tied!

Pass rope
over the hand.

Rope Release ▲

Have someone tie a large handkerchief around your wrists. Then a length of soft rope is passed between the wrists. The ends of the rope are held by the spectator. Tell him to hold on to them so you cannot escape. Ask someone to throw a large scarf over your wrists.

As soon as the scarf covers your wrists you use your wrists to move the loop of rope for-wards. If the wrists have been tied fairly loosely this is quite easy to do.

Now pass the loop through the handkerchief towards your hand. Pull the loop right through and pass it over your hand. All you have to do now is give a sharp tug and the rope will slip out of the handkerchief at the back. As you give the tug toss the scarf off your hands.

The rope is now free but your hands are tied.

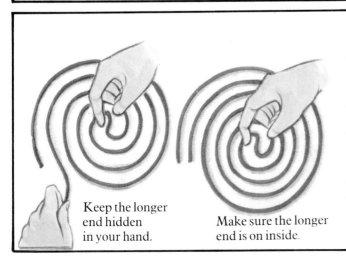

Keep the longer
end hidden
in your hand.

Make sure the longer
end is on inside.

Slippery Spiral

Fold the string in two so that any end is about thirty centimetres longer than the other.

Roll it into a spiral as shown.

Someone puts their finger in the centre again. You pick up both ends of the string and pull— and the string comes away from the finger.

Again you lay the string down in a spiral. Before you do this make sure that the longest end is on the inside. When the spiral is com-pleted the long string is laid down around the outside of the spiral to give it another turn. This time the finger will be trapped!

27

Magic of the Mind

Turn your back while someone picks up the fruit.

Ask her to raise one of the fruits to her forehead and concentrate hard on it.

Your friends will be amazed when you pick the right fruit.

Fruity Thoughts▲

Place an apple in someone's hand. Put an orange in his other hand.

Now turn your back. Ask him to pick either one of the fruits, hold it next to his forehead and concentrate hard on it.

Tell him to put his hand down. Turn back to face him and you can tell the fruit he chose.

The secret is quite simple. All you have to do is look at his hands. The palest one will be holding the fruit he is thinking of. This is due to all the blood draining from that hand while he was holding it to his forehead.

Capital Cities►

The spectators call out the names of several capital cities from around the world. The magician writes down each name on a piece of paper. Each paper is dropped into a box.

Someone picks out any paper from the box and the name of the selected city is read out. The magician then calls attention to an envelope that has been hanging in full view throughout the performance. When the envelope is opened there is a large card inside. On the card is written the name of the city that would be chosen.

This trick is very effective but the secret is quite simple. Choose the name of a popular capital—let us assume that you choose Paris. Write this on the card and seal it in the envelope. Put the envelope in full view.

Ask the spectators to call out the names of capital cities. You appear to write these down on slips of paper. What you really do is to write the same name on each slip. In this case you would write 'Paris'. So no matter which slip is chosen it is bound to read 'Paris' and the prediction in the envelope is always correct.

In the News⬥

Cut out a column of print from a newspaper. This column must have exactly thirty five lines.

Write the seventeenth line on a piece of paper. Put the paper in an envelope. Seal the envelope.

You are now ready to show a baffling mind-reading miracle.

Hand the envelope to someone in your audience for safe keeping.

Give the newspaper and a pencil to someone in your audience. Ask that person to cross out between five and ten lines from the top of the column.

He is then to cross out from one to five lines from the bottom of the column.

Now ask him to count how many lines are not crossed out. Whatever number he gets he is to add the two digits together. So, if he counts twenty four unmarked lines he adds the two and the four to make six.

Tell him to add to this number the number of lines he crossed out at the bottom of the column. He is now to count that number of lines down from the first unmarked line. Ask him to put a tick against the line on which he finishes the count.

When the envelope is opened the audience will be amazed to see you knew in advance which line would be chosen.

Magic with Money

◄**Heads or Tails**

Someone spins a coin on the table. Even though you are blindfolded you can always tell whether the coin has fallen with the head or tail up.

The trick is quite simple—but it is also baffling. You used the nicked coin from the last trick. When this coin falls with the nick underneath it makes a different noise than when it falls with the nick uppermost. All you have to do is spend a few minutes listening to the coin beforehand so you can tell the difference in sound between the two sides.

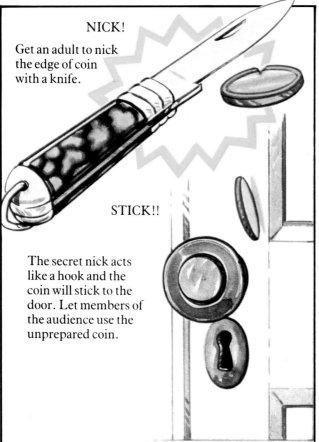

NICK!

Get an adult to nick the edge of coin with a knife.

STICK!!

The secret nick acts like a hook and the coin will stick to the door. Let members of the audience use the unprepared coin.

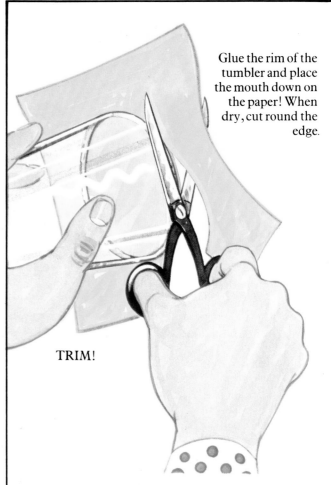

Glue the rim of the tumbler and place the mouth down on the paper! When dry, cut round the edge.

TRIM!

It's a Stick-up▲

Get an adult to nick the edge of a small coin with a knife. Do not do this yourself, you may cut yourself. You can now do a super trick.

Casually show the coin to your friends and then press it against a wooden door. The secret nicks acts like a hook and the coin will stick to the door.

Remove the coin and secretly exchange it for an unprepared coin of the same value, hidden in your hand (you will have to practise this). Hand the unprepared coin to someone in your audience and let them have a go. They will not be able to do it.

Only you know that two coins are used.

The Coin and Tumbler ▲

Put a layer of glue around the rim of a glass tumbler. Place the tumbler mouth down onto a sheet of paper. When the glue has dried trim the paper so there is just a neat round piece covering the mouth of the tumber.

Place a sheet of paper on your table. This must be the same type of paper glued on the tumbler. Place the tumbler mouth down on it. With a handkerchief and a coin you are now ready to perform this trick.

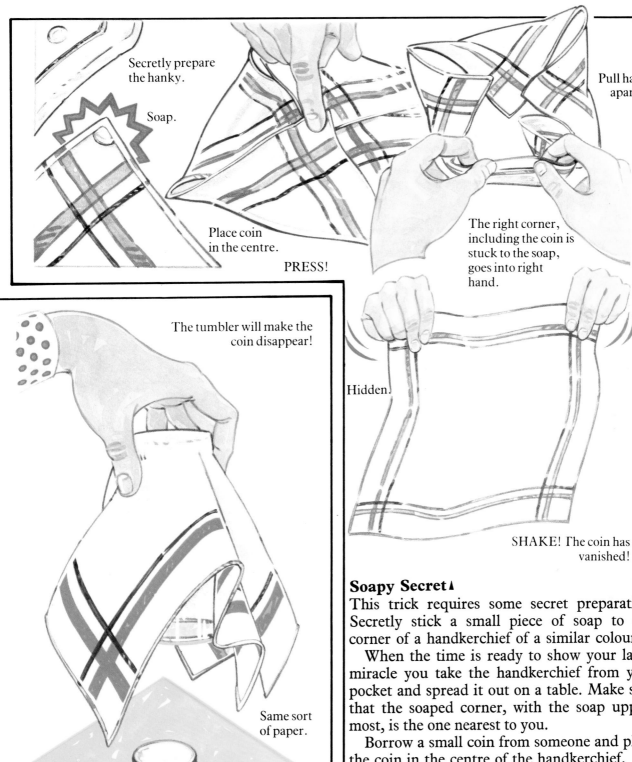

Secretly prepare the hanky.

Soap.

Place coin in the centre.

PRESS!

Pull hands apart.

The right corner, including the coin is stuck to the soap, goes into right hand.

Hidden.

The tumbler will make the coin disappear!

Same sort of paper.

SHAKE! The coin has vanished!

Show the coin and place it on the paper. Cover the tumbler with the handkerchief. Then lift it through the handkerchief and place it over the coin.

Remove the handkerchief and the coin has vanished. It is really hidden under the paper attached to the tumbler.

To make the coin come back put the handkerchief over the tumbler once again. Lift the tumbler through the handkerchief and the coin is back on the table!

Soapy Secret

This trick requires some secret preparation. Secretly stick a small piece of soap to one corner of a handkerchief of a similar colour.

When the time is ready to show your latest miracle you take the handkerchief from your pocket and spread it out on a table. Make sure that the soaped corner, with the soap uppermost, is the one nearest to you.

Borrow a small coin from someone and place the coin in the centre of the handkerchief.

Lift the soaped corner of the handkerchief and place it on the coin. The soap must be touching the coin. Now bring the other corners into the centre, one at a time.

Press on the corners with one finger. Say: 'The coin is in the centre of the handkerchief'.

Now take hold of the handkerchief with both hands on the open left corner nearest to you. Pull your hands apart quickly. The left corner of the handkerchief goes into your left hand and the right corner into your right hand along with the coin.

Shake the handkerchief. The coin has gone.

Silken Sorcery

The right hand secretly pulls hanky from sleeve.

Bring both hands together and produce the hanky!

Handkerchief from Nowhere ▲

The magician shows that both his hands are empty, pulls up his sleeves, and then produces a coloured handkerchief from nowhere.

The handkerchief is first hidden in a fold in your left sleeve just above the elbow.

Show both hands empty. With the left hand pull up the right sleeve to show there is absolutely nothing hidden. Now the right hand pulls up the left sleeve. At the same time the right hand secretly picks up the handkerchief.

Bring both hands together and produce the handkerchief.

Houdini Handkerchief ►

In this trick you use a coloured handkerchief to represent the famous magician, Houdini. (Silk handkerchiefs are best.) This handkerchief is prepared by having a short length of cotton attached to one corner. The thread should have a large knot tied at its end. The audience do not know about this.

Place the Houdini handkerchief into a glass tumbler. The tumbler represents the jail. Make sure that the thread is hanging outside the tumbler at the back.

On top of the Houdini handkerchief put an ordinary white handkerchief. This is the jailer. Another white handkerchief is draped over the mouth of the tumbler. An elastic band is placed around it to hold the handkerchief in position.

It is obvious to your spectators that the coloured handkerchief is well and truly trapped.

Reach under the white handkerchief and secretly pull on the thread. This will pull the Houdini handkerchief out of the glass. Now take hold of the corner of the coloured handkerchief and keep pulling downwards. It looks as if the handkerchief is being pulled through the bottom of the glass.

Hand the covered tumbler to a spectator and allow him to remove the elastic band, and the covering white handkerchief. Inside the glass is the other white handkerchief but there is just a space where the coloured handkerchief was a moment before. It seems that the coloured handkerchief must have escaped through the bottom of the glass. But the spectator finds it to be completely solid.

Attach knotted thread to 'Houdini'.

Cover the tumbler containing two hankies with another hanky and secure with an elastic band.

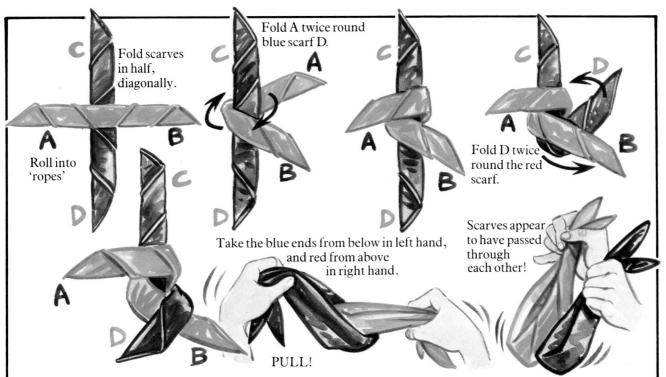

Fold scarves in half, diagonally.

Roll into 'ropes'

Fold A twice round blue scarf D.

Fold D twice round the red scarf.

Scarves appear to have passed through each other!

Take the blue ends from below in left hand, and red from above in right hand.

PULL!

Solid through Solid

For this trick you will need two large silk scarves. It is best if they are both the same colour. But you will find the trick easier to learn if you use two different colours, like red and blue, to start with.

Fold each handkerchief in half diagonally and then roll it up into a 'rope'.

Place the red one across the blue one as shown in the picture.

Hold the handkerchiefs together at the centre in your left hand.

Place your right hand under the handkerchief and take the left end of the red handkerchief. Wrap the red handkerchief twice around the blue one. Follow the pictures carefully.

Now take the bottom end of the blue handkerchief and wrap it twice around the red one.

Take the ends of the red handkerchief from above in your right hand.

Take the ends of the blue handkerchief from below in your left hand.

Slowly pull your hands apart and the handkerchiefs appear to pass through one another.

Spectators think that the Houdini hanky must have escaped through the bottom of the glass.

Reach under the hanky and secretly pull the thread until you can take hold of 'Houdini.'

TUG! TUG!

33

Baffling Tricks

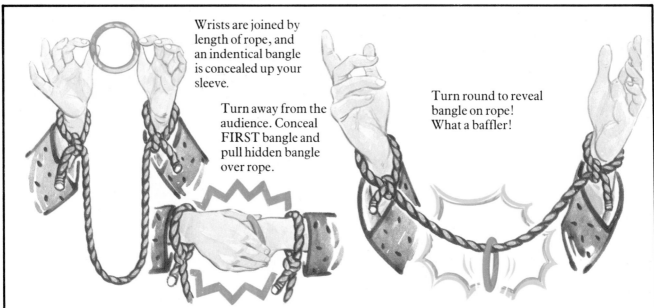

Wrists are joined by length of rope, and an indentical bangle is concealed up your sleeve.

Turn away from the audience. Conceal FIRST bangle and pull hidden bangle over rope.

Turn round to reveal bangle on rope! What a baffler!

The Baffling Bangle ▲

A spectator is handed a length of rope. He is asked to tie one end of the rope around your right wrist and the other around your left wrist.

You then show a large ring. The spectators can examine this ring if they wish.

You turn around for just a second. When you turn back to face the audience once again the ring is seen to be hanging on the rope! Your wrists are still tied securely.

The secret of the trick is quite simple. You have two rings. The rings can be made of anything as long as they are identical.

Before your performance one of the rings is placed on your arm. It is then pushed up your sleeve out of sight It is the other ring that is shown to the audience.

As you turn your back you simply slip the first ring into an inside pocket. Now pull the hidden ring from the sleeve and on to the rope.

Impossible Lift ►

The magician folds a newspaper and lays it across the top of two plastic tumbers. He then places his wand between the tumbers. When he lifts the wand the newspaper and tumblers come up as well, as if magnetised.

This trick is done with a small piece of wire that is never seen by the audience. Bend the wire into a U-shape. It is a good idea to use the wand to help you do the bending as it will then be shaped to the correct size.

Use some sticky tape to fix the wire to the newspaper.

The newspaper can be shown casually and the wire will not be seen. Fold the newspaper into a long packet with the wire on the side facing you.

Put the tumblers together and then lay the newspaper on top of them. The paper must be positioned so one prong of wire goes into each tumbler.

Push your wand in between the tumblers near the base. Now raise the wand up to the newspaper and the whole lot can be lifted.

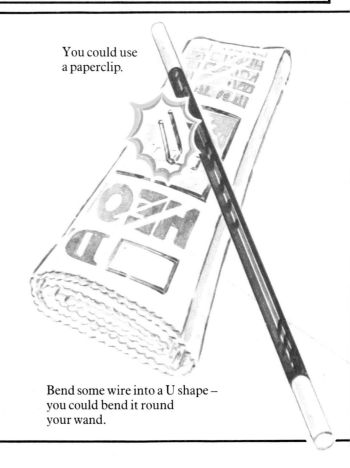

You could use a paperclip.

Bend some wire into a U shape – you could bend it round your wand.

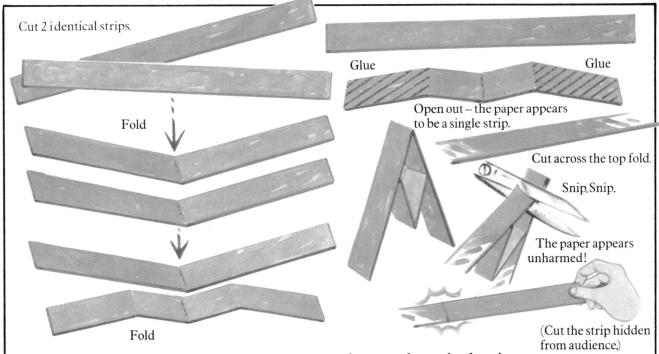

Cut 2 identical strips.

Fold

Fold

Glue Glue

Open out – the paper appears
to be a single strip.

Cut across the top fold.

Snip, Snip.

The paper appears
unharmed!

(Cut the strip hidden
from audience.)

Unharmed Paper ▲

The magician shows a strip of paper. He folds it in half and then cuts a large piece from its centre. But when the paper is opened out it is seen to be whole again.

The strip of paper you use for this is really two strips glued together. Each strip should measure about three centimetres wide by about forty centimetres long.

Fold both strips in half and then open them. Take one of the strips and fold it into an M shape as shown in the picture.

Glue the strips together where shown and you are ready to perform.

If you hold the strip opened out it looks quite ordinary. Fold it in half, making sure the centre folds go in opposite directions as shown.

Cut across the top fold. Open out the paper again and it looks as if you have restored it by magic. When you show the strip at the end of the trick make sure the cut piece is on the side away from the audience.

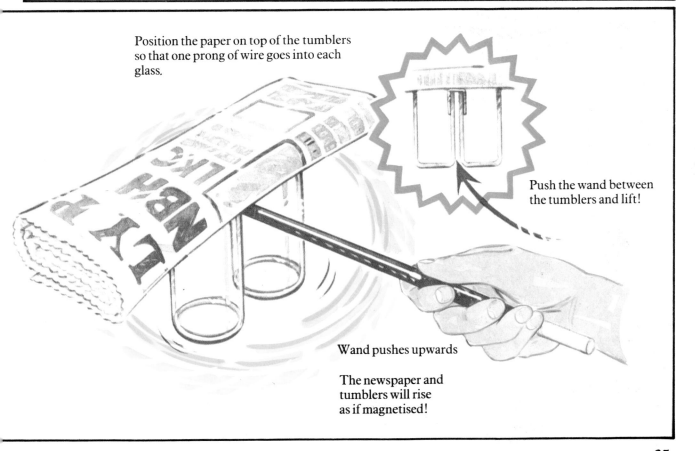

Position the paper on top of the tumblers so that one prong of wire goes into each glass.

Push the wand between the tumblers and lift!

Wand pushes upwards

The newspaper and tumblers will rise as if magnetised!

Magic with Movement

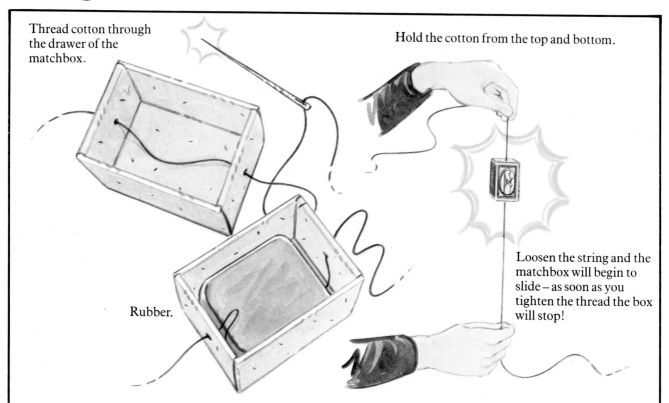

Thread cotton through the drawer of the matchbox.

Rubber.

Hold the cotton from the top and bottom.

Loosen the string and the matchbox will begin to slide – as soon as you tighten the thread the box will stop!

Obedient Matchbox▲

Make a small hole in each end of the drawer of a matchbox. Thread thin cotton through the holes. Now put a small block of wood or a pencil eraser into the drawer. This must go on top of the thread. Put the drawer back into the box and you are ready to perform.

Hold one end of the cotton in one hand and the other end in the other hand. Hold the cotton taut. Keeping the cotton taut, position your hands so one is above the other. The matchbox is on the cotton between your hands. It should be near the top of the cotton.

Loosen the cotton slightly and the matchbox will begin to slide down it. As soon as you pull the cotton tight the matchbox will stop.

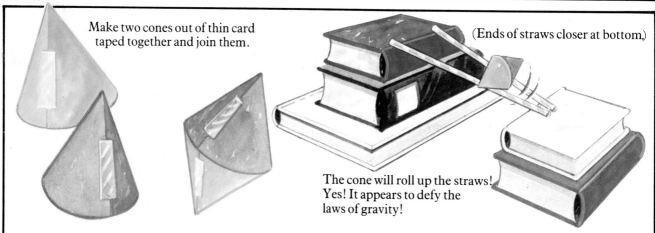

Make two cones out of thin card taped together and join them.

(Ends of straws closer at bottom.)

The cone will roll up the straws! Yes! It appears to defy the laws of gravity!

Diamond Roll▲

Take two pieces of thin card and roll them into a cone shape. A piece of sticky tape along one edge will hold the cones in shape.

Now use some more sticky tape to fix the cones together, mouth to mouth, so they form a cone-shaped diamond as shown in the picture.

Arrange some books on the table and lay two strong straws or thin strips of wood across them as shown. The ends of the straws should be closer at the bottom than they are at the top This is important. This is the secret upon which the whole trick depends.

Put the diamond cone on the straws at the bottom of the slope. Much to everyone's surprise it will roll to the top of the slope!

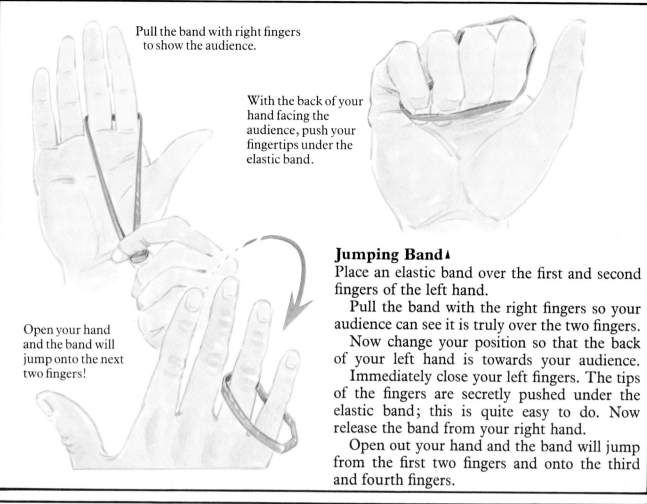

Pull the band with right fingers to show the audience.

With the back of your hand facing the audience, push your fingertips under the elastic band.

Open your hand and the band will jump onto the next two fingers!

Jumping Band ▲

Place an elastic band over the first and second fingers of the left hand.

Pull the band with the right fingers so your audience can see it is truly over the two fingers.

Now change your position so that the back of your left hand is towards your audience.

Immediately close your left fingers. The tips of the fingers are secretly pushed under the elastic band; this is quite easy to do. Now release the band from your right hand.

Open out your hand and the band will jump from the first two fingers and onto the third and fourth fingers.

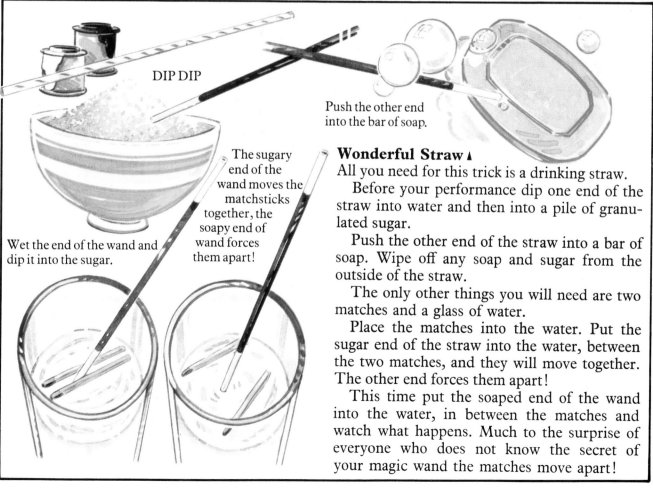

DIP DIP

Push the other end into the bar of soap.

The sugary end of the wand moves the matchsticks together, the soapy end of wand forces them apart!

Wet the end of the wand and dip it into the sugar.

Wonderful Straw ▲

All you need for this trick is a drinking straw.

Before your performance dip one end of the straw into water and then into a pile of granulated sugar.

Push the other end of the straw into a bar of soap. Wipe off any soap and sugar from the outside of the straw.

The only other things you will need are two matches and a glass of water.

Place the matches into the water. Put the sugar end of the straw into the water, between the two matches, and they will move together. The other end forces them apart!

This time put the soaped end of the wand into the water, in between the matches and watch what happens. Much to the surprise of everyone who does not know the secret of your magic wand the matches move apart!

More Magic of the Mind

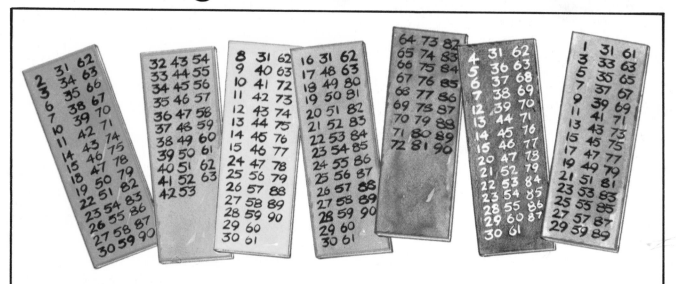

Numbered Thoughts ▲

Ask a spectator to think of any number between one and ninety. With the aid of the special magic cards shown on this page you can tell the spectator what number he is thinking of.

All you have to do is to ask the spectator to take the cards. He is then to hand back to you all the cards that have his chosen number on.

When he gives the cards back to you all you have to do is look at the number at the top left hand corner of each card. Add these numbers up and your answer will be his number.

As soon as the selected object is pointed at, your friend moves his right foot.

Mind Reading Miracle ▲

While you are out of the room someone thinks of an object in the room. He tells everyone what it is and then calls you back.

When you come back into the room someone points at different things around the room. As soon as he points to the object that was chosen you tell him to stop.

You know which item was selected because one of the people in the room is your confederate. As soon as the selected object is pointed to he moves his right foot slightly. That is your agreed signal. Immediately he moves his foot you know that the object being pointed at is the one chosen.

Ask the audience to note the numbers on the dice.

Glued dice.

Dice Deception ▲

Glue two dice inside one end of a large matchbox. Position the dice so that a five and a three are uppermost. You will also need two other dice to do this trick.

Show the two loose dice and say you are going to make a prediction. Write on a piece of paper the figure eight. Do not let anyone see what you have written. Fold the paper up and ask someone to look after it.

Open the matchbox at the opposite end to the glued dice. Drop the two loose dice into it.

Give the matchbox a shake. Now open it at

Before your act put your prepared slips of paper into one side of the bag.

The spectators put their slips into the other side.

◄ Thoughts in Harmony

You ask members of the audience to write the names of famous people on pieces of paper and then to drop the papers into a cloth bag. As the papers are dropped into the bag each spectator calls out the name of the person he has written.

You are now blindfolded and a spectator is asked to pick any slip of paper from the bag. You name the name written on the paper!

The secret is really quite simple. The bag is doubled as shown in the picture. Perhaps you can get your mother to make one for you. Before your act you write the name of a famous person on several slips of paper. These are put into one side of the partitioned bag.

During your performance the spectators drop their slips of paper into the other side of the bag. When you ask someone to pick one out you make sure that his hand goes into the prepared side of the bag. Whatever slip he picks will bear the name of your person.

To make sure that someone calls out the person you have written you can always get a friend in the audience to write a slip of paper with your chosen name on it.

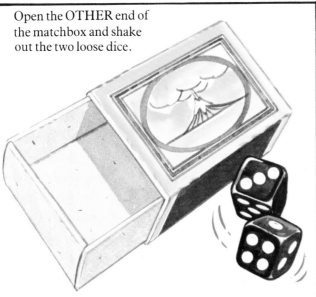

Open the OTHER end of the matchbox and shake out the two loose dice.

the prepared end so that the two glued dice become visible. Allow your audience to see the dice. Ask them to note the two sides (five and three) that are uppermost. Close the box.

Ask the person who is holding the piece of paper to open it. At the same time you casually open the matchbox at the unprepared end and tip out the two loose dice. Ask one of the spectators to call out the total of the two dice seen in the box. He will say 'eight'. Ask the person who is holding the paper to read out what it says. He reads 'eight'.

You are truly a great mind reader.

Ask the spectators to throw two dice separately.

Mathematical Mystery ▲

Hand someone two dice and ask him to throw each separately on the table. Your back is turned.

Now ask him to double the number shown on the first dice.

To his answer he must now add five.

This answer has to be multiplied by five.

He is now to add on the second number he threw. When he has done that he must tell you his answer. As soon as he does so you mentally subtract twenty five from it. The answer you arrive at will consist of two numbers. The first number will be the number thrown by the first dice. The second number will be the number showing on the second dice.

Strange Secrets

Rub soap over the back of the paper.

The spectator writes a word on the paper resting on the sheet of glass.

Read the word on the glass, then rub it clean while pretending to 'build up' electricity.

Crystal Clear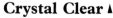

Secretly prepare a sheet of writing paper by rubbing soap all over one side. You will also need a small sheet of clear glass.

Hand the glass to a spectator and rest the paper on it. The soaped side must be downwards. Give the person a pencil and ask him to write down any word he likes.

When he has finished writing he folds up the paper and puts it in his pocket. The glass is handed back to you and you rub it with a cloth.

You say that this is to build up electricity.

You now place your fingers on the spectator's forehead. 'To allow the electricity to flow from one person to the other.' Then you surprise everyone present by announcing the word.

What really happens is that the soaped paper will cause an impression of the word to appear on the glass. You can read this quite easily. That is how you find out what the word is. Rubbing the glass is really to clean off the writing so no one else will see it!

Necklace of Mystery ▶

Arrange thirteen coins on a table in a figure nine formation as shown in the picture.

Ask a spectator to think of any number above five. He is not to tell you what it is.

While your back is turned he is to start counting from the tail of the mystic coin necklace. When he reaches the upper part of the nine he continues counting around the circle until he reaches the number he is thinking of.

He now has to reverse his counting. The coin on which he stopped is counted as one and he continues counting around the circle in the opposite direction. When he reaches the final number he is to make a mental note of the coin at which he has stopped.

You now turn around and point to one coin. Although you had no idea of the spectator's number it is the coin on which he stopped! The trick is mathematical. Whatever the number chosen the selected coin will always be the same one. It is marked in the picture which shows the counting procedure if the number twelve had been chosen.

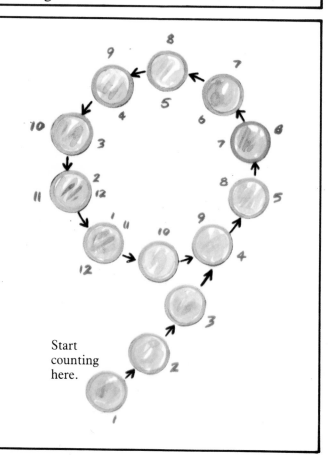

Start counting here.

TAP! TAP!

◄ Time Will Tell

Ask someone to think of any hour between one and twelve. He must not tell you what number he is thinking of.

You now tap a clock face with a pencil. Your friend is to count the taps starting from the number he is thinking of. So, if he is thinking of four he will count the taps as five, six, and so on. When he reaches twenty he is to call out 'Stop'. Much to his surprise you are now pointing the pencil at the very hour of which he is thinking.

All you have to do is to tap against any of the numbers on the first seven taps. The eighth tap must be on the twelve, the ninth on eleven and so on going the wrong way around the clock. The trick works by itself. When your friend reaches the number twenty you will be pointing at the hour he thought of.

Worlds Apart ►

Place two ping pong balls on a table about five centimetres apart.

When you put your finger on the table in between the two balls they will roll apart, much to the amazement of your friends.

What your friends do not notice is that you secretly blow at your finger. It is your breath, not magic, that make the two balls separate.

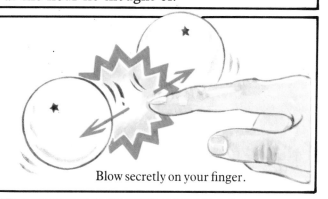

Blow secretly on your finger.

◄ Haunted Whistle

You show your audience a whistle hanging from a piece of string. When you ask the whistle questions, it answers them with a whistle—one whistle for yes, two whistles for no. Or the whistle can be made to give the answers to simple sums.

The secret of how the whistle works is a special tube hidden under your clothing. You will also need another whistle and a small rubber bulb. The tube and the rubber bulb can be bought from a chemist's shop.

Push one end of the rubber tube into the bulb. Push the whistle into the other end of the tube. Place the bulb under your armpit and allow the tube to run down your sleeve. The whistle should be positioned just inside the opening of the sleeve.

It is this secret whistle, not the one the audience can see, that makes the noise. To blow the whistle you simply bring your arm in towards your body and squeeze the rubber bulb.

You should be a little way away from your audience when doing this trick so they cannot tell exactly where the noise is coming from.

SQUEEZE!

Squeeze the bulb secretly with your arm.

(The bulb should be hidden under your clothes.)

Miracles of Magic

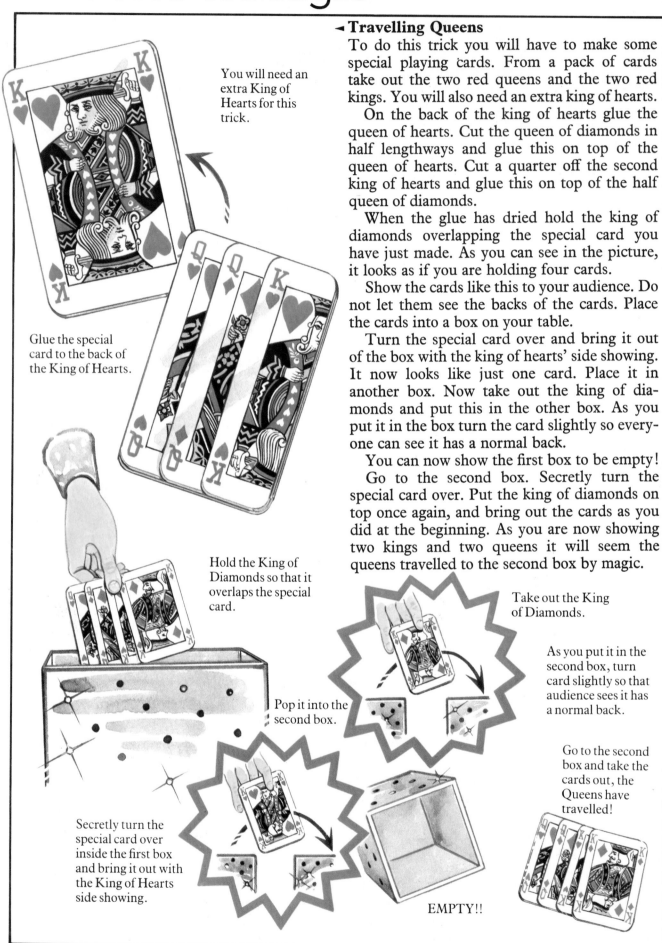

You will need an extra King of Hearts for this trick.

Glue the special card to the back of the King of Hearts.

Hold the King of Diamonds so that it overlaps the special card.

Pop it into the second box.

Secretly turn the special card over inside the first box and bring it out with the King of Hearts side showing.

EMPTY!!

Take out the King of Diamonds.

As you put it in the second box, turn card slightly so that audience sees it has a normal back.

Go to the second box and take the cards out, the Queens have travelled!

◄ **Travelling Queens**

To do this trick you will have to make some special playing cards. From a pack of cards take out the two red queens and the two red kings. You will also need an extra king of hearts.

On the back of the king of hearts glue the queen of hearts. Cut the queen of diamonds in half lengthways and glue this on top of the queen of hearts. Cut a quarter off the second king of hearts and glue this on top of the half queen of diamonds.

When the glue has dried hold the king of diamonds overlapping the special card you have just made. As you can see in the picture, it looks as if you are holding four cards.

Show the cards like this to your audience. Do not let them see the backs of the cards. Place the cards into a box on your table.

Turn the special card over and bring it out of the box with the king of hearts' side showing. It now looks like just one card. Place it in another box. Now take out the king of diamonds and put this in the other box. As you put it in the box turn the card slightly so everyone can see it has a normal back.

You can now show the first box to be empty!

Go to the second box. Secretly turn the special card over. Put the king of diamonds on top once again, and bring out the cards as you did at the beginning. As you are now showing two kings and two queens it will seem the queens travelled to the second box by magic.

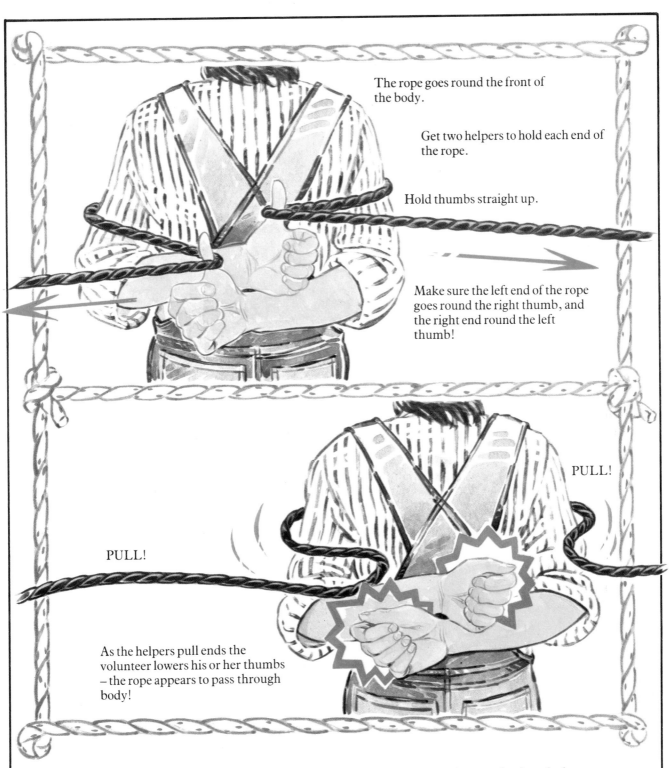

The rope goes round the front of the body.

Get two helpers to hold each end of the rope.

Hold thumbs straight up.

Make sure the left end of the rope goes round the right thumb, and the right end round the left thumb!

PULL!

PULL!

As the helpers pull ends the volunteer lowers his or her thumbs – the rope appears to pass through body!

Through the Middle ▲

For this trick you will need an assistant. You will also need a very long length of rope.

Ask two people to come up and help you. Allow them to examine the rope. They can pull it to make sure there are no secret joins.

One person stands on one side of the stage. The other person is on the other side. Your assistant stands in the middle.

Stand behind your assistant. Put the centre of the rope over her head and to her front.

You now seem to wrap the rope around your assistant's body before handing the ends to the two people you have asked to help.

What really happens is that your assistant lifts her thumbs behind her back. The rope goes round the thumbs and not all the way around the body as the audience think.

Make sure that the left end of the rope goes round the right thumb and the right end goes around the left thumb.

The helpers now pull on the rope. Your assistant secretly puts her thumbs down—and the rope appears to go right through her body.

This is quite a spectacular trick. It is well worth putting in some extra practice.

Professional Secrets

Show the box to the audience while holding the flap in place.

Move the flap over and produce what's inside!

◄ Miraculous Handkerchiefs

In this effect you first show a box empty then you produce from it a number of coloured handkerchiefs and ribbons.

To do this you will need a special box.

First get an ordinary shoe box or something similar. Paint the outside with bright colours so it looks magical. Paint the inside black.

Get a sheet of card, also painted black, and tape this into the centre of the box as shown. You now have a flap that can be placed against the front or the back of the box. While it is in one of these two positions cut it down so its edge is at the same height as the edge of the box.

Put some handkerchiefs and ribbons into the box. Push the flap over so it covers the handkerchiefs.

By holding the box on the edge where the flap is positioned you can show it quite casually. It looks as if it is empty.

Place it on your table, move the flap across to the other side, and then produce the handkerchiefs and ribbons.

Pull your hands apart and the envelope travels from your right to left hand!

Cotton threaded through two holes in envelope.

PULL!

PULL!

Blob of wax or gum.

Air Mail Letter ▲

The magician holds a letter in his right hand. His hands are well apart. Slowly the letter floats mysteriously through space and into his left hand. Immediately the letter is passed out for examination but there is nothing suspicious.

This remarkable trick is accomplished by means of a thread. It must match your clothes so that it is almost invisible.

Two small pin holes are made in the top of the envelope and the cotton is threaded through them. One end of the cotton is attached to the bottom corner of the envelope with a blob of wax or a small piece of chewing gum. The other end of the cotton is wound around your right forefinger.

Insert the left thumb into the loop of cotton and draw your hands apart slowly. This will make the envelope leave the right hand and move across to the left.

As soon as it reaches the left hand secretly pull the wax off the envelope. The cotton can now be pulled away completely and the envelope handed out for examination. No one is likely to notice the two small holes through which the cotton was threaded.

On with the Show

Act of Magic

You now know the methods of enough tricks to enable you to perform several acts of magic.

Select a few tricks you like and which you think an audience will like.

Try to keep the tricks in your act both entertaining and mysterious.

Start your act with a trick that is quick, bright and baffling.

Save your best trick as the last one in your act. It will enable you to go out on a big finish.

Get yourself a table on which you can place all the properties you need before the start of your act.

Have a cover made for the table so your act looks really professional.

Try to learn a few jokes to brighten up your act.

Always look at your audience, speak clearly so everyone can hear what you are saying, and enjoy what you are doing. If you do not enjoy it, you cannot really expect your audience to enjoy it, can you?

Above all make sure that you know exactly what you have to do for each trick. You must also know exactly where to pick up each item needed for a trick. You will then give an error-free performance. This will help to enhance your image as a great magician.

     *   *   *   *   *

Don't try to learn too much at once. Learn just a few tricks. When you can do them well you can go on to learn a few more.

Don't perform any trick, no matter how simple, in public until you have rehearsed it thoroughly.

Don't repeat a trick at the same performance. If someone says 'Do it again', politely refuse or show them a completely different trick.

Don't bore your audience. They may not like magic as much as you do. Please remember that. Keep your shows short and entertaining and you will be asked back to do some more.

Don't tell anyone how the tricks are done. People are bound to ask but please do not reveal the secret of any trick. A large part of the fascination of magic is the mystery that surround its methods. If you explain how a trick is done, the bubble of mystery is burst.